You (All-Inclusive)

Katherine Bird

BookLeaf Publishing

Presentation by *BookLeaf Publishing*

Web: www.bookleafpub.com

E-mail: info@bookleafpub.com

ISBN: 9789357442947

First edition 2023

For me, ironically. I hope I'm proud.

ACKNOWLEDGEMENT

First of all, thank you to my family. I would be nowhere without your support. Thank you for teaching me how to cook, speak, live, and feel enough to write in the first place.

Thank you to Fee. Your love of poetry has inspired and continues to inspire many. I gratefully and cheerfully await the time we get to work together again.

Thanks to Robin, who I irritated most of the time I was writing this. Thanks to Aren, who I irritated the rest of the time. And thanks to Dys, who would never admit to any time I've irritated her because you're too lovely for that. Kai, Ev, Rin, Josh and many others— thank you all, too, for both being supportive and being my friend. And inspiring maybe a couple of these. Don't worry about it.

And finally, thank you, Estella. I simply wouldn't be myself without you, and I love you more than anything. If you buy a copy of this yourself, I'll give you the money from the palm of my hand.

PREFACE

The following poems contain swearing and themes or mentions of blood, death, sex, alcohol and drugs.

palpitations

the night we met in your kitchen
swiftly followed by a blanket of stars
as we exchanged our gentle promises
just endless repeated chants of
"we should, we should, we should"
tomorrow couldn't come soon enough
the sun flees from the clouds, too easy
to fall for someone like you more everyday
now that i have your contact information
how can i be shy when you open my heart?
i can't wait to love you

throw it

adrenaline flushes all your loose movements red
music crowns you like royalty, in charge til
you're dead
sending the dart board across the room an
air-kiss
chasing you higher so you'll laugh when i miss
this
your eyeshadow glimmers as you take another
shot
i hope you're paying for these drinks because
i'm not
i look into your eyes and think i'd give half my
lifespan
to ride in your old car or bus or boat or slow
tram
the wild way your brain moves gives my
floating head whiplash
i'd board that bullet train though i know you'd
crash

part two past ten

you're not an owner
not a minimalist either
i've never owned much

so without believing it
you think you're mine
and i know you want to be

Fried Egg with Spring Onion

Office cubicles, sunshine
Clear skies, stack of paper
My lunch spins in the microwave
Your clouds replace my steam
Smooth light blue tiles on the bathroom wall
You promised, even then, to come pick me up
Now where are you?

garden

green leaves, brown pot
on my desk next to
clear cup, cream drink
£4.70 straw free

"every other day"
i was allowed my
sugar, like cake
nuts and vanilla
purple like you
for my own garden
i don't like tapioca
so your tea waters
my plants and me

last time i came
for my fertiliser you said
"try these pearls if you
like blueberry muffins"

i'll heat cups of water
steep my dead leaves
and if i am as i
hardly ever am
entirely honest with myself

though i choose to love you
you make me wish
i was better
at boiling milk

outlive me

falling in love with you is miserable
"unreciprocated" is all i've known
though i know you're not lying, i still
feel like you aren't being honest either
was any of this meant to happen to us?
i wouldn't mind if you hated me, but
you seem to enjoy our shared time
and i can't work that through just yet
your heart feels wrong in my hands
who— no, what are you holding onto?

She messaged me,

what's your favourite food what's your favourite
colour
where do you like to go out with your friends
where do
you live how old are you how old do you say
you are at
the bar have you ever overdosed is this where
you like
to hang out the most why don't i get you some
you give
me your number and i'll pay cheers see you next
friday?

then she told me to never talk to her again crazy
bitch
maturity suits your features you have such nice
hair
god i want you by my side for as long as you'll
be
i've never met someone like you i swear
good morning baby how'd you sleep
sorry i'm so late i was at work
sure i'm down today
nah not now
not really
u up?

no i promise babe
why are you asking me that
labels are overrated seriously no
seriously what are you talking about
look i'm sorry you feel like that but i haven't
what do you expect me to beg like a fucking dog
no please i'm sorry i promise it won't happen
again
come over let's just talk

you ever taken some of this before
apparently you can meet god
breathe in

i've missed you
what do you mean
wait aren't you seeing this
i'm not scaring you
don't leave yet let it hit let me
can we stay here please just a while
just a while how many times have we jumped
it's so pretty here just us just us just us please
what i feel for you is the strongest i've ever felt
i love you i lvoe you i love you i love i love
please please
for you anything lord knows god knows
please
i promise i won't leave
never never never never never

yeah my last ex blocked me she was crazy
what's your favourite food

0.0%

thank you for believing i would amount
to a total of nothing.
o dandelion root, not mine,
now i have outdone you,
what do you have to say
for yourself? i win.

Mr Miniature Coffin, Who's it For?

who was that?
i don't know her
but i think i recognised her
seems like someone i knew once
but her face is so unfamiliar still
form so young
and a smile

when i learnt to recognise her
she moved in the same day
now she sleeps in my chest when she can
and you are the reason she can't sleep

i can't stand it anymore
the way you ignored her
i know damn well i was yelling
my head aches as it unravels
could a new justice make her happy?
when will i finally get it?

i was seven
trying to reach heaven
how old were you?

Contact Formats

You told me immortal nemeses are usually accidents // once // maybe because dedicating my existence to you wasn't my intention // you feel bad // you shouldn't // you wish I was better // I don't know which one of us I wish was dead // you're invested in my penance because you're not like me // I'm like you // but I'll still crawl into your skin // your hearts are transparent in my eyes // you can't hate me because you'd never let anyone else see inside your soul // when I say I hate you I mean me // you'll write my memoir because you know no one else could be you // but that's not fair // you'd say we met one November // I know how many days it's been since we crashed again // tell me // you're the only one that needs me // they need you too // you know we have the same brain // the last survivors of the same home // say it // say it // I'm in your blood // just like you're in mine

Breathe / Breeze

There is no water here
Heavy breathing, dry mouth
Squeak of shoes on the floor
taunting me knowing I'll never catch up
to the hair swimming through the open air
in the shadowed stairwell
in the coolest corridors
I swallow my lump of a tongue and
reach out and grab your ponytail
and pull.

Your head slides like a surf board
your blood leaves a trail for my eyes to follow
like sea foam you are everything and nothing at
once
then nothing, unrisen sun's blue light cast on
your features
painting you into an aquarium I gaze into like a
ball
of crystal destined to show me nothing at all.

Your skin is paler than mine now
And the hallway is silent
my knife lays by your side
the companion I failed to be

your smile isn't here to bring the sun
and the moon has long left the currents alone
to splash along the shore unsure.
Always about the ocean, weren't we?

my cup of tea

using you wasn't my intention
your face smiles despite the
circumstances i land us in always
i was always going to do this
why did it have to be to you?

OURS

1	You
2	Missing
3	Since last week
4	Since forever

5	I'm back at school now
6	Where you leave me waiting
7	Where I confront your remains
8	Where we would all laugh on the stairs

9	I found your bones under the west wing
10	Please just come back in ten minutes or
less
11	I promise I'll forgive you for everything
12	Before the excavation team gets back
from lunch

We Missed You!

I lost you like a button
thread worn from use
once you'd pushed mine
one hundred too many times
Like a plane flying over Canada
Like my favourite marble
Like an album made of false photos
Like my grandma's dog
who bit me once
who I never saw again.
I lost you last week
When you sent me your location
I turned off my phone and went home.

a teenage girl is hell

i'm staring at a photo i'm staring at your
shirt sleeve cropped elbow skin so pale
now glowing in my colourless universe
pink grey ballerina hiding in a harsher
beat and a producer tag every morning
i thought neither of us had mothers i
thought we shared that hole us just us
anything will bring me back to you
but you're standing there instead palms
glued to your sides your cinched waist
cotton candy perfume with a french
name only you and your sister know
if there's no truth in closeness between
us you're the best at it i'm sick of it all
if i put your heels on anyone would fall

perfume

pardon? no, what did you say?
almost unintelligibly, you repeat the curse;
your habits won't break like this, i say.
you know that. you do.
if happiness is all there is for us, even if
you can't walk you should crawl—
then, shouldn't you be running by now?

your eyes are as broken as mine. do you
ever wonder why we can still see each other,
silent as we are, unfixable as we are?
pale beach, waves roll, encased in purple,
the irreparably fractured world you see is
only the darkest shards.
are you just silent or listening?

would you let me destroy you?
will you always eat again eventually?
i know what i want to say to you, and i
wish it wasn't something you need to hear.
i flicker before your eyes, more like a glitch than
a candle.
are you seeing me on purpose?

don't reach out, don't let go, i can't control
you—
inferiority rules you, aren't we the same by
now?
a virtual orchestra screams the same chorus as
your words echo,
i'm alright. i will survive.
a fading decided sacrifice, i wonder—
which of us will succeed first in our
self-inflicted martyrdom?

honesty

i asked you to hold my hand
you reached across the universe
into my chest
and closed your fist tightly around my heart

everyone i know has called me a puzzle,
an enigma, hard to crack

i am the most open person i have ever known
my ribs are already cracked open
my guts spill out every time my mouth opens
you can see my heart beating out of my chest
why haven't any of you worked me out yet?

no raincoat

i am not the sun you call me
you know i am too covered for that
in thousands of layers i'd rather not unwrap,
sorry
i'm always sorry i can't live with the hardship
for me the gap between loving and being loved
is far too hard to consider crossing
do you understand, really?

you say it's alright
but i have no umbrella to give
to help you weather our fallout

i am the hurricane katrina
you heed no warning
though love has never relaxed me
i don't mind if you undress in front of me
no sane person keeps wet clothes on

Two Mornings After

I thought heaven was white
but you make it feel so golden
like honey and coins and my hair
even though you don't know the colour
I know yours
I will always know yours

Everything I've ever done for you I would do
a thousand times over, and everything I've
ever done to you is my biggest regret.
Now my bedsheets smell like you and I
wish I died in your arms yesterday
when you were here and your love
burnt me like an ice cube

I'm fine with having nothing
as long as you have nothing, too
I don't mind if you use me like a tool
I do too. And I can't die for myself in my room
can I

seven stories high

25

your voyage and return bring me
riches for my rags; this quest was
equal parts comedy and tragedy.
i am overcoming your monster;
i ask no further questions, i am reborn.

Thank Light

if my heart could speak, it'd have your voice.
if i could choose my last words, they'd be your
names.
if i can't die with you, i'd rather die alone—
though, i'll really always die with you, honestly.

you are safety. you are all i know.
you've witnessed more of me than i think i ever
will.
you touch something and it becomes love.
i wish i could touch you— just waiting for next
spring.

you credit me for your creation. how could i hate
myself
when you make me the most proud i've ever
been of anyone?
how could i hate myself anyway, when you
made me too?
how are you love? how are you, love?

i would choose you over anything.
you are all that i will pray for—
i'll say, please, god,
any star but that one.
that one, that love's mine.